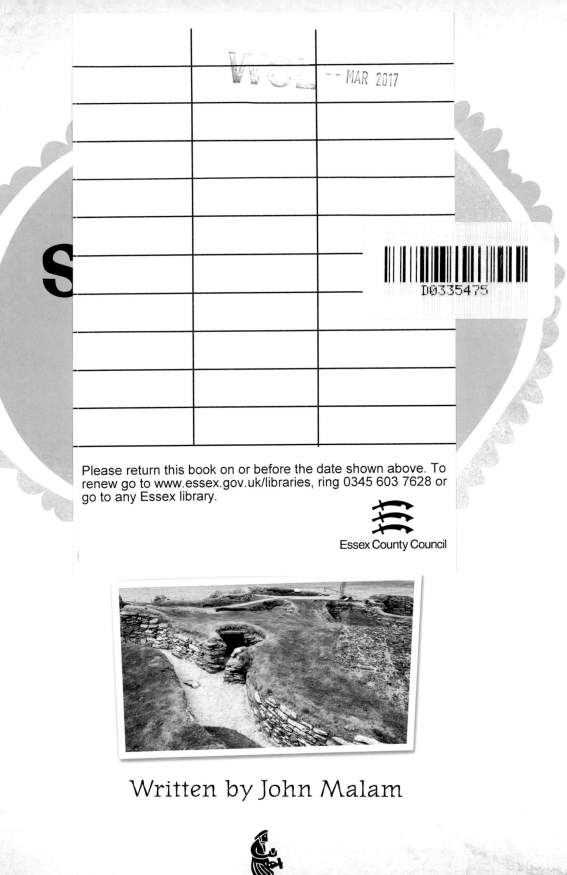

Written by John Malam

CONTENTS

STONE, BRONZE AND IRON

How do you decide how old an object is? You can look at how it is made, and what material it is made from.

   In 1816, a man called Christian Thomsen was putting on a display of ancient artefacts at a museum in Copenhagen, Denmark. There were hundreds of objects, but they weren't organised into a system. Thomsen decided that as the simplest material, the stone objects would have come first. They were the oldest objects. He had objects made of bronze and iron left. He put the bronze items next in the display, as bronze-making was an earlier discovery than iron-making.

The Three Age System in Britain

Stone Age
(800,000 years ago to 2300 BCE)
Tools, weapons and other objects were
made from pieces of stone, especially flint.

Flint
arrowhead

Bronze Age
(2300 BCE to 800 BCE)
Stone was replaced by metal. Copper was the first metal used.
Then came a harder metal called bronze.

Iron
dagger

Iron Age
(800 BCE to 43 CE)
Bronze gave way to iron, an even harder metal.
The Iron Age ended in 43 CE, when the Romans invaded Britain.

Bronze
axe

The Stone Age is divided into three periods:

1. Old Stone Age or the Palaeolithic
800,000 to 10,000 years ago
The first people lived in Britain.
Much of this period is called
the Ice Age, because sheets of
ice covered most of the land.

2. Middle Stone Age
or the Mesolithic
10,000 years ago to 4000 BCE
The ice melted and groups
of hunter-gatherer people
moved across Britain.

3. New Stone Age
or the Neolithic
4000 BCE to 2300 BCE
The time of the first
farmers and villages
in Britain.

WHAT IS PREHISTORY?

Archaeologists have found evidence of human life in Britain dating back around 800,000 years. From this, they have been able to build up a picture of how human life has changed over all that time.

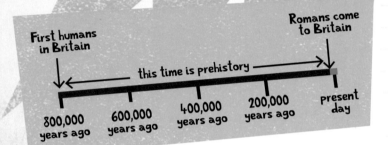

First humans in Britain | this time is prehistory | Romans come to Britain

800,000 years ago — 600,000 years ago — 400,000 years ago — 200,000 years ago — present day

Before history

When the Romans came to Britain in 43 CE they brought written language with them. They wrote down and recorded things that happened, so the time after their arrival is known as 'history'. Before this, no one in Britain could write and events were not recorded. Archaeologists call this time prehistory.

The word 'pre' means 'before'. So, the word 'prehistory' means 'before history'.

Investigating artefacts

Since the earliest times, humans have made things. Archaeologists call these objects 'artefacts'. Prehistoric people made artefacts such as axes, pottery bowls, and jewellery. When the artefacts were broken, they were thrown away. Sometimes they were lost, or buried in the ground on purpose.

Archaeologists dig up prehistoric artefacts and investigate them. It's one of the main ways they find out about the past.

Prehistoric digging tool made from a deer antler

ANCIENT HOMES

All around Britain we can find evidence of people who lived on these islands thousands of years ago. From the remains of their settlements we can learn about their daily lives, their families, beliefs, diet, work, and even travels.

SKARA BRAE

 WYRE

Skara Brae

LOCH TAY CRANNOG

Replica Iron Age house at Loch Tay

The Stone Age site at Windmill Hill

FLAG FEN

Carn Euny Iron Age village

WINDMILL HILL

DURRINGTON WALLS

CARN EUNY

BRITAIN'S FIRST FARMERS

For thousands of years, prehistoric people found food by moving from place to place, eating animals that they could catch by hunting and collecting plants that grew in the wild. This was the hunter-gatherer way of life – but it was coming to an end.

Neolithic people were farming far away like these so they worked the land.

Neolithic sheep were like these Soay sheep, found on islands off the west coast of Scotland.

From hunters to farmers

About 6,000 years ago, people arrived in Britain from Europe. They crossed the sea in small boats, bringing seeds and farm animals with them. They brought the idea of farming to Britain.

Slowly, Britain's hunter-gatherer people changed the way they lived. Instead of roaming the land, they settled down and became farmers. They grew crops and kept farm animals. Farming marked the start of a new period in British prehistory, called the Neolithic or New Stone Age.

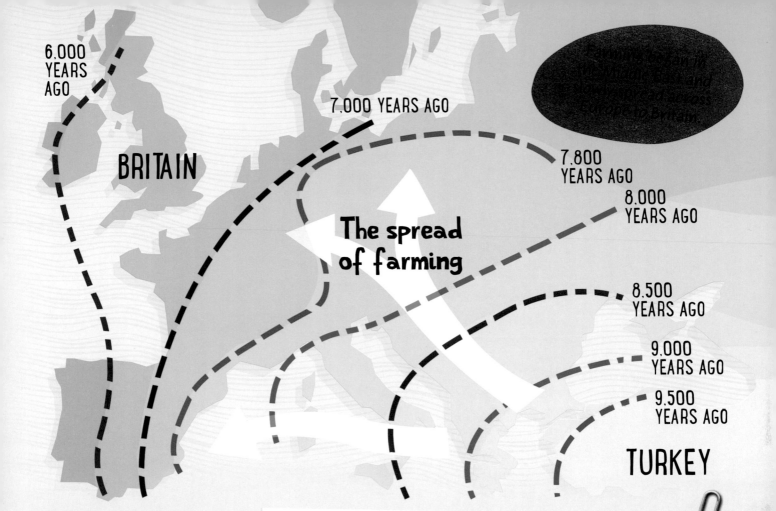

6,000
YEARS
AGO

7,000 YEARS AGO

BRITAIN

7,800
YEARS AGO

8,000
YEARS AGO

The spread
of farming

8,500
YEARS AGO

9,000
YEARS AGO

9,500
YEARS AGO

TURKEY

Farming began in
the Middle East and
spread across
Europe to Britain

The first villages

At the start of the Neolithic period, most of Britain was covered in forests. The first farmers had to clear the land of trees to make space for their fields. The change from hunting to farming meant a change in the way that prehistoric people lived. To look after animals and tend the crops, they settled down to live in one place. The first villages were a few houses grouped together close to the farmers' fields.

Stone axe

The first farmers used stone axes to cut down trees. The sharpest axes were made from pieces of flint, shaped to give them cutting edges. The axes were held in wooden handles.

Archaeologists have experimented by making their own modern flint axes. In one experiment it took more than 11,000 blows from a flint axe to cut down a tree.

Stone axe made from flint

AN AWESOME DISCOVERY

Just off the north coast of Scotland are the Orkney Islands. In the winter of 1850, a great storm blew in from the sea and battered them. On the largest island the storm washed away part of a big sand dune, uncovering something buried inside it...

After the storm

A few days after the storm, local people made an incredible discovery. They found walls poking out from inside the sand dune. As they cleared away the sand, they uncovered the remains of small houses, built of stone. They'd never seen anything like them, and nor had anyone else.

We call the village Skara Brae. This comes from 'Skerrabra' – the old name for the sand dune that had buried the prehistoric village.

From above, you can still see the shapes of the houses, and just how close they are to the sea.

A buried village

Many years later archaeologists excavated the site. As they removed the sand, a cluster of about ten stone houses was revealed. The houses stood close together and were joined by narrow passages, like tunnels. People could move from house to house without having to go outside.

Skara Brae is the best-preserved Neolithic village in Europe.

A passageway between two of the houses.

Archaeologists believe the houses belonged to a village that was about 5,000 years old. It had been built in about 3100 BCE, in the Neolithic period. There were probably more houses at one time, but the sea has washed them away.

Another village

Skara Brae was not the only Neolithic village on Orkney. In 2006, archaeologists found a new village, on the tiny island of Wyre. Like Skara Brae, it also had stone houses, and is at least 5,000 years old.

STONE HOUSES

Today, we can only imagine what it must have been like to live inside a Skara Brae house. It was a small space for a family. The open fire and solid walls would have made it dark and smoky, but it would have been warm and safe in the wild Scottish islands.

Inside a Skara Brae house

The houses at Skara Brae were all built from pieces of flat stone. They were square-shaped with rounded corners, and the walls were about a metre thick. A low doorway was the only way inside.

Each house had one room made from rough stone walls. Inside the house these were covered with clay, which dried and went hard. The clay helped to keep heat inside the house, and also stopped the wind from blowing through gaps in the stones. There were no windows in the walls to let in light or air.

In the centre of the room a fire burned dried seaweed, animal dung and driftwood from the beach. The fire gave light, kept the house warm, and was used to cook food.

Around the edge of the room...

The flat stones were easy to stack on top of each other.

On the roof

Today, the Skara Brae houses have no roofs – they disappeared long ago. When prehistoric people lived in the houses, the roofs might have been made from thatch or turf, laid onto a frame made from whale bones or wood. A hole in the centre of the roof would have let smoke from the fire escape from the house.

Comfy seat?

It wasn't only the house walls that were made from stone, flat stones were used to make furniture, such as cupboards and seats, too.

The sides of beds were made from large pieces of flat stone. Beds were like open boxes and were probably filled with moss, heather, straw and animal fur to make them cosy and warm.

DINNER TIME

When archaeologists excavated Skara Brae, they found lots of evidence for what people living there ate. It was like looking into a 5,000-year-old dustbin!

Food from the land

The people of Skara Brae were farmers and fishers. The sandy soil was easy to dig and plough, and in the summer months the villagers grew wheat and barley. When harvested, these grains were ground into flour, which was baked into bread. The grains might also have been brewed into beer.

The community kept cattle, sheep and pigs that provided milk and meat. Their wool and skins were used for clothing, and their bones were made into tools. Red deer and wild boar were hunted for their meat.

Mounds of rubbish

The houses were surrounded by rubbish. Archaeologists found huge dumps of limpet shells, animal and fish bones piled up against the house walls. There was so much rubbish, the houses were almost buried under it!

Limpets might have been 'emergency food', only eaten when there was little else to eat.

Food from the sea

Some people went out in small boats to catch fish, others searched the shoreline for food. Archaeologists found bones from cod and coley, as well as masses of limpet shells.

Fish food

Set into the floor of each house you can see small boxes made from stone. It's thought these were 'fish tanks' where live limpets were kept. The limpets could have been used as bait when people went fishing out at sea for cod and coley. If so, this would explain why so many thousands of limpet shells were found.

People ate crabs and oysters as well as seabirds and birds' eggs. One of the birds eaten was the great auk – a big, flightless bird that must have been easy to catch. The great auk is now extinct. When they could catch it, people ate seal meat, and if a whale was washed ashore, its meat would have provided enough for a feast.

LIFE AND DEATH

What was it like to live at Skara Brae? There may only have been a few families there at any one time, and everyone must have known each other and worked together.

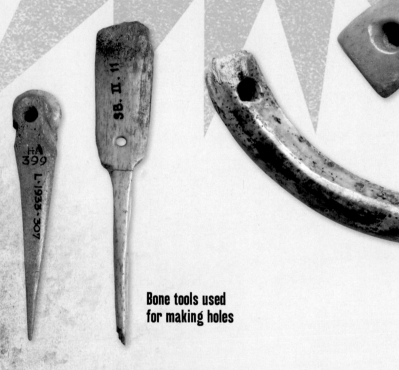

Pendants made from an animal tooth and a horn

Bone tools used for making holes

The Skara Brae people used animal bones, teeth, tusks and horns to make tools, pendants, and pins for fastening clothes.

Making things

All the tools and objects that the people at Skara Brae needed, they made themselves. Archaeologists have found all sorts of objects in and around the houses. The people in the village made cutting tools from stone. They made stone axes and knives which had sharp cutting edges.

Among the other objects found are beads and pendants that were made from shells, sheep bones, and teeth from cows and whales. Animal bone was used to make hairpins, needles and fasteners to hold clothing together. Clothes were made from animal fur and skins were turned into leather.

Mystery objects

Archaeologists have found carved stone balls at Skara Brae. They're about the size of apples and would have taken a lot of skill to carve. They're a complete mystery as no one can work out what they were for.

Carved stone ball

Houses of the dead

Archaeologists found the skeletons of two women buried under the floor of one of the houses. They were the only human skeletons found at Skara Brae. So, where was everyone else buried? One idea is they were buried in a chambered tomb that has not been found, or has been washed away by the sea.

The end of Skara Brae

Skara Brae village was lived in for 600 years, from about 3100 BCE until about 2500 BCE. Archaeologists found signs that the village was abandoned in a hurry. They believe that a disaster, such as a great storm, may have struck the village. Whatever happened, the people moved away, and the village was forgotten.

A Neolithic tomb on Orkney, Scotland. Perhaps when people died at Skara Brae, they were buried inside a tomb like this one.

A PREHISTORIC MEETING PLACE?

It's called Windmill Hill, but you won't see a windmill there today. In fact, at first it might seem like an ordinary low, grassy hill. But if you look a little more closely, you'll see the remains of deep ditches dug long ago by prehistoric people.

Windmill Hill might have been a busy place 4,500 years ago.

Broken circles

Windmill Hill is in the county of Wiltshire in south-west England. At the start of the Neolithic period, prehistoric people dug three deep ditches around the top of the hill. Soil from the ditches was piled up on the inside of the ditches to make high banks of earth. There might have been a wooden fence on top of the bank, to make it even higher.

The ditches were roughly circular – but had lots of breaks or gaps in them. These were made so that people could walk through to reach the middle. The gaps are known as 'causeways' and so sites like this are called causewayed enclosures.

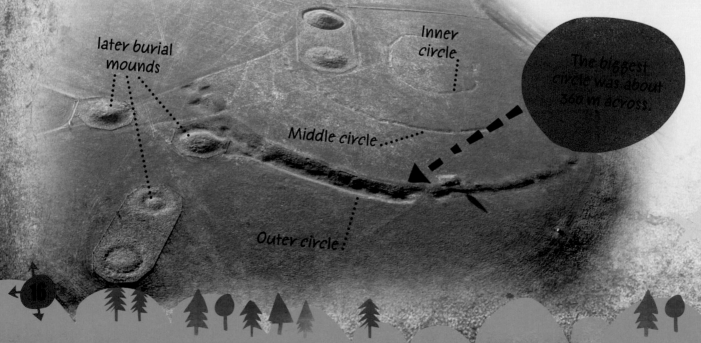

later burial mounds

Inner circle

Middle circle

Outer circle

The biggest circle was about 360 m across.

What was Windmill Hill used for?

When archaeologists excavated Windmill Hill, they found lots of broken pottery, pieces of flint, animal and human bones and ash from fires. They also found objects, such as stone axes, carefully buried in the ditches.

These finds made them think the top of the hill was used as a meeting place. People may have gathered for feasts and ceremonies, settled arguments and made friends, and exchanged farm animals and everyday goods.

Britain's oldest pottery

The first pots were made by hand from pieces of soft clay, then baked in a fire until they were hard. The pots were used for cooking food and heating liquids. Archaeologists call this type of Neolithic pottery 'Windmill Hill pottery', because this was one of the first places they found it. It was made about 5,000 years ago.

There are about 70 prehistoric places like Windmill Hill in Britain.

A NEOLITHIC VILLAGE

There are lots of Neolithic sites in the south of Britain, such as Windmill Hill (see page 16), but where did everyone live? Archaeologists had been searching for traces of Neolithic villages in the south of England for years, but without success.

Missing piece

The long search finally ended in 2004 when archaeologists discovered the remains of a Neolithic village in the county of Wiltshire. It was lived in about 4,500 years ago.

Finding a Neolithic village in this part of England was like finding the missing piece in a jigsaw. Archaeologists could then investigate how Neolithic people in this part of Britain would have lived.

Archaeologists named the village 'Durrington Walls', after another Neolithic place. Here you can see the floor of a house in the villlage.

Replica houses

Archaeologists have built replica Neolithic houses, like the ones you can see here. They are based on evidence found at the Durrington Walls village. The walls are made from wattle and daub (hazel sticks covered in a thick layer of white chalky mud), the floors from beaten chalk, and the roofs are covered in thatch. Inside is a hearth in the middle of the floor where a fire burns.

The Neolithic houses at Durrington Walls were like these modern replicas.

Durrington Walls vs. Skara Brae

The houses at Durrington Walls were completely different from the ones far to the north at Skara Brae. Rather than being made from stone, the Durrington Walls houses were made from wattle and daub.

Skara Brae was a small village with only a few houses, but the Durrington Walls village may have been massive. Some archaeologists think it had hundreds of houses, which would make it the largest Neolithic village in Britain.

This is how archaeologists think the Neolithic village at Durrington Walls might have looked.

A FESTIVAL VILLAGE?

As prehistoric people changed to a farming lifestyle, many small villages would have appeared across Britain. But Durrington Walls is bigger than the other sites, and archaeologists have found some clues as to why...

Plenty to eat

Archaeologists have found masses of animal bones at Durrington Walls, mostly from young pigs. Instead of being random bones, all mixed up, a lot of the bones were still connected. The only way that could have happened is if the bones were thrown away with meat still on them – the meat would have held the bones together.

If people could afford to throw meat away, they must have had plenty of food to eat. What was going on? The best answer is that Durrington Walls village was a place where people enjoyed feasts, with more than enough food to go around.

Meat from pigs was eaten by Neolithic people all across Britain.

'Festival village'

The village is only about 3 km away from the famous stone circle of Stonehenge. Archaeologists think that a great festival took place at Stonehenge, at sunset on Midwinter's Day (21st December) to mark the end of winter and the beginning of spring. For the new farming communities, it was a time to celebrate the coming of warmer weather and the start of the growing season after the dark, cold days of winter. It may be that people came to Durrington Walls in time for the great festival.

Winter
feasting

The pig bones are a clue to when feasts were held at Durrington Walls. Piglets are usually born in February and March, and the bones found at Durrington Walls were from pigs just a few months old. This makes archaeologists think the feasts were held in the winter, and that Durrington Walls was not lived in all year round like a normal village.

An artist's reconstruction of Durrington Walls in the middle of winter. It must have been a lively place for the villagers going to Stonehenge for the Midwinter festival.

FLAG FEN

When archaeologists found wood poking out from the side of a ditch at Flag Fen, they could hardly imagine what they were about to uncover – wood, wood and more wood!

A Bronze Age boat made from a hollowed-out tree trunk. Archaeologists had to carefully dig it out of thick, wet clay.

Prehistoric platform

Flag Fen is in the Fens – an area of wet, marshy land in the east of England. About 3,000 years ago, Bronze Age people built a massive wooden platform there, made from 250,000 pieces of wood laid on top of each other in layers.

As well as the strange platform, they had pushed about 60,000 upright wooden posts into the soft, waterlogged ground. The posts were in five long lines, running from dry land to the platform out in the wet land.

This is how archaeologists think the Flag Fen timber platform and lines of posts might have looked in the Bronze Age.

Waterlogged

Now that archaeologists have investigated the site, it is important to keep it waterlogged. Once the wood is exposed to the air, it immediately starts to dry out and decay. If this was allowed to happen, the site would be lost forever! An artificial lake and sprinker system have been created to keep the wood under water, so the air can't get to it. If any wood is taken from the site, archaeologists spray water over it to keep it wet.

The side of a Bronze Age boat. You can see it still looks like a tree trunk.

Bronze Age boats

The Fens were so wet in the Bronze Age that people used boats to travel across them. They were made from hollowed-out tree trunks. People used paddles to move them through the water.

A sacred place

Archaeologists found thousands of objects carefully placed into the wet ground. There were bronze swords, spears and daggers, clay pots, and masses of animal bones. Some of the metal weapons had been deliberately bent before being placed in the water.

Archaeologists think the Flag Fen platform was a sacred place, where people gathered for ceremonies. They think prehistoric people imagined the watery world beneath their feet was the land of the dead or the home of water spirits. The objects they placed into the water were their gifts to those who dwelled there.

Oldest wheel

One of the oldest wooden wheels in Britain was found at Flag Fen. It's made from three planks of wood joined together.

The wooden wheel, as it was found at Flag Fen.

SECRET PASSAGES

Across Cornwall are many Iron Age settlements. Carefully constructed beneath some of them are stone passages and chambers. But what did ancient people use these secret places for?

Carn Euny

About 500 BCE, Iron Age people built a settlement at Carn Euny. The houses were small, round and probably made from a mixture of wood and turf, with thatched roofs. In about 50 CE, the wooden round houses were rebuilt in stone. It is the remains of these that we can see today.

There were about ten houses in the village. They were grouped close together and some shared walls with each other. The stone houses were oval with very thick walls. There was one main room in the middle, and smaller rooms built into the walls.

A reconstruction of an Iron Age house at Carn Euny.

Underground secret

At the same time as the first houses were built at Carn Euny, Iron Age people built a long, narrow passage, just below the surface of the ground. The passage was about 20 m long, lined with stone and with a roof covered by big, flat stones. At the end of the passage they built an underground room.

The roundhouses in Carn Euny village, seen from the air.

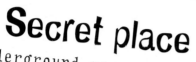

Secret place

Underground passages like the one at Carn Euny are found only in Cornwall. No one really knows what they were for. Some people say they were used as shelters in times of trouble. Others think they were used like cellars, where food and other goods could be stored.

The end

Like all Iron Age communities in Britain, the people of Carn Euny were farmers. They grew crops, kept farm animals, and made their own things such as clothes, and pottery. The village was lived in for about 800 years before it was abandoned.

LIVING ON WATER

In parts of Scotland and Ireland, some prehistoric people in the Bronze Age and Iron Age built their houses on water, at the edges of lochs and lakes. They were built from wood, on manmade floating islands called 'crannogs'.

In Ireland, some big crannogs are called 'royal crannogs'. They might have been where important people lived.

This replica shows how a crannog was like a floating island, surrounded by water.

Building a crannog

It took a lot of wood to build a crannog. The first thing to do was to push lots of long posts down into the soft mud at the bottom of the lake. They had to be long enough to poke up above the surface of the water. These posts became the 'legs' or stilts of the crannog island. The more legs it had, the stronger the crannog would be.

When all the legs were in place, the builders started to build the crannog platform or floor. This was made from wood, fixed to the legs above the water level. When the platform was made, one or more wooden roundhouses were built on top of it. A wooden bridge connected the crannog to the land, so people could come and go between the two.

A modern crannog

At Loch Tay, Scotland, archaeologists found a 2,600-year-old Iron Age crannog. When they excavated it, they found a butter dish with Iron Age butter still in it! The cold water of the loch had preserved the butter.

There's now a modern replica of the crannog built on Loch Tay. It's based on the real Iron Age crannog in the loch.

Why build crannogs?

It's thought that crannogs were built in times of trouble. If danger approached, people could leave the land and take shelter in their island homes. Because they were surrounded by water, they were easier to defend than houses built on land.

The only way on and off a crannog was by a narrow bridge that joined it to the land.

DISCOVERING THE PAST

Most of Britain's prehistoric settlements disappeared long ago. Only a few are still standing above the ground for us to see today, such as the stone houses at Skara Brae and Carn Euny. What about the rest?

Eyes in the sky

Archaeologists have used planes, balloons and kites to take photographs from the air. Now they're using drones or UAVs (unmanned aerial vehicles) to take aerial photos and videos. These small flying machines give archaeologists a bird's-eye-view of a site, helping them to clearly see its layout, which is hard to do at ground level.

Drones are like mini helicopters. This one has a camera underneath it.

Looking for clues

All across Britain are the buried remains of prehistoric settlements. Hidden beneath fields and under today's towns are the traces of farms and villages from the Stone, Bronze Age and Iron Age periods. If you look at the ground closely as you walk you might spot mounds or dips that indicate prehistoric sites. Here are four methods archaeologists use to find ancient remains:

1 Cropmarks
Archaeologists fly over fields and take photographs. If there is something buried, it might show up as marks in the grass or crops. The marks are called 'cropmarks'. By looking at photographs of cropmarks, archaeologists can tell what is under the field.

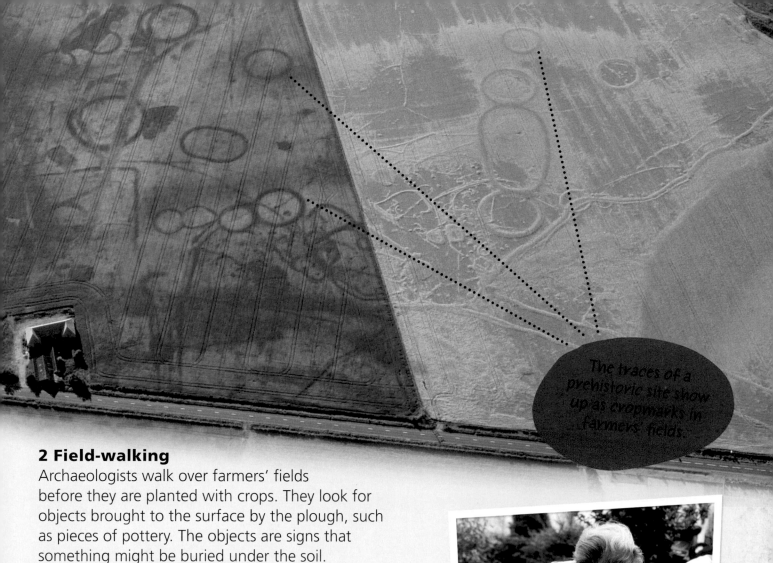

The traces of a prehistoric site show up as cropmarks in farmers' fields.

2 Field-walking

Archaeologists walk over farmers' fields before they are planted with crops. They look for objects brought to the surface by the plough, such as pieces of pottery. The objects are signs that something might be buried under the soil.

3 Excavation

Only when archaeologists dig into the ground will they know for certain what's there. This is called 'excavation'.

4 Seeing what's there

Archaeologists use machines that can 'see' into the ground. The machines make maps and archaeologists can then work out what's there.

Living in the past

Another way to find out about the past is through 'experimental archaeology'. This is when archaeologists build houses using the same tools and methods as prehistoric people. They plough fields, grow crops, cook food, make pots and weave cloth, just as people did in prehistoric times. It helps us all to learn about the past.

An archaeologist flaking and shaping a piece of flint. This is experimental archaeology.

SETTLEMENTS IN NUMBERS

95,000 pieces of flint found at Windmill Hill

250,000 pieces of wood in the Flag Fen platform

1,300 smashed pots found at Windmill Hill

10 stone houses at Skara Brae Neolithic village - there might have been more

2,000 crannogs in Ireland

1 wooden wheel found at Flag Fen - the oldest wheel in Britain

60,000 upright wooden posts in the Flag Fen rows

50,000 hours of work to dig the ditches and build the banks of soil at Windmill Hill

5 long rows of wooden posts at Flag Fen

600 crannogs in Scotland

10 stone houses at Carn Euny Iron Age village

70 causewayed enclosures discovered in Britain - so far

168 long timber posts pushed into the bottom of Loch Tay to hold up a replica crannog

GLOSSARY

abandoned When something is left behind on purpose.

archaeologist (say: are-kee-ol-o-jist) A person who finds out about the past, often by digging things up.

bronze A metal made by mixing copper and tin. It's harder than copper, but softer than iron.

burial mound Stone or timber structures covered in soil, used mainly for burying the dead.

causewayed enclosure A type of monument built in the Neolithic period with circular ditches and banks of soil. There were gaps or breaks in the ditches and banks, for people to pass through.

cereal A type of grass that produces grains used for food, such as wheat, barley and oats.

chambered tomb A place with rooms or chambers where the dead were buried in the Neolithic period.

crannog A manmade island in some lochs and lakes in Scotland and Ireland.

cropmark A pattern in a crop or a grassy field showing the outline of buried remains.

dung Animal droppings.

flint A type of stone that was chipped into shape to make tools such as axes, arrowheads and scrapers.

fogou (say: foo-goo) An underground passage found at some prehistoric places in Cornwall. It means 'cave'.

henge A type of prehistoric place made in the Neolithic period. It was a circular enclosure surrounded by a ditch and a bank of earth.

hunter-gatherer A person who lives by hunting wild animals and gathering wild plants.

Mesolithic (say: mez-o-lith-ik) The Middle Stone Age period, about 10,000 years ago to 4000 BCE.

Neolithic (say: nee-o-lith-ik) The New Stone Age period, about 4000 BCE to 2300 BCE.

Palaeolithic (say: pal-e-o-lith-ik) The Old Stone Age period, about 800,000 to 10,000 years ago.

prehistory The time in human history before writing began.

roundhouse A circular house made from wattle and daub, wood and thatch.

stone circle A type of monument built in the Neolithic or Bronze Age with standing stones placed in a circle.

thatch A type of roof covering made from straw.

Three Age System A way of dividing prehistory into three parts: Stone Age, Bronze Age and Iron Age.

wattle and daub Building material made by weaving thin branches (wattles) together and covering with a thick layer of mud mixed with straw and animal dung (daub).

Understanding dates

- The letters 'BCE' stand for 'Before Common Era'.

- The letters 'CE' stand for 'Common Era'.

- BCE dates are counted backwards from the year 1. CE dates are counted forwards from the year 1. There was no year 0.

- Some dates have a 'c.' in front of them. This stands for 'circa' (say: sur-ca), which means 'about'. These dates are guesses, because no one knows exactly what the real date is.

INDEX

Published in paperback in 2017 by Wayland
Copyright © Hodder and Stoughton, 2017

All rights reserved.

Author: John Malam
Consultant: Mark Bowden, Historic England
Editor: Annabel Stones and Liza Miller

Historic England is a Government service championing England's heritage and giving expert, constructive advice.

ISBN: 9781526303431
10 9 8 7 6 5 4 3 2 1

Wayland
An imprint of
Hachette Children's Group
Part of Hodder & Stoughton
Carmelite House
50 Victoria Embankment
London EC4Y 0DZ

An Hachette UK Company
www.hachette.co.uk
www.hachettechildrens.co.uk

Printed in China

Cover illustrations © Lee Hodges
Cover image © Shutterstock
images © Historic England Publishing:
3tl, 4, 5ml, 5bl, 7b, 16, 17, 19b, 20b, 21r, 25t, 29t
images © Francis Pryor: 18, 22t, 23t
illustrations by Kerry Hyndman: 5, 7, 12, 17, 24

Picture credits:
Corbis 25b, 26; Dreamstime 19t; Museum of London 31, 3br; National Museums Scotland 14, 15t; RCAHMS 13b, 15b; Science Photo Library 27b, 29b; Shutterstock 1, 55, 5mr, 6, 8, 9, 10, 11, 13tl, 13tr, 20t, 27t, 28l; Vivacity 22b, 23b